JUST IN TIME!

PALM SUNDAY AND HOLY WEEK SERVICES

Robin Knowles Wallace

Abingdon Press
Nashville

JUST IN TIME!
PALM SUNDAY AND HOLY WEEK SERVICES

This book is printed on acid-free paper.

Library of Congress Cataloging-in-Publication Data

Wallace, Robin Knowles.
    Palm Sunday and Holy Week services / Robin Knowles Wallace.
        p. cm. — (Just in time!)
    Includes bibliographical references and index.
    ISBN 0-687-49778-7 (binding: adhesive, perfect : alk. paper)
        1. Palm Sunday. 2. Holy Week. 3. Worship programs. I. Title. II. Series: Just in time! (Nashville, Tenn.)

    BV91.W35 2006
    264—dc22

                                                                                        2006003135

06 07 08 09 10 11 12 13 14 15—10 9 8 7 6 5 4 3 2 1
MANUFACTURED IN THE UNITED STATES OF AMERICA

To Sister Joanmarie Smith for teaching me about

the Triduum and much more.

CONTENTS

Contents

INTRODUCTION

Holy Week is one of the most vital times of the Christian year. Beginning with Palm Sunday, we are immediately plunged into the drama of Jesus' last week on earth in human form—cheered into the city on Sunday, then by Friday, tried and condemned like a common criminal. This book is a collection of prayers, dramas, music suggestions, and services for Palm/Passion Sunday, Holy (or Maundy) Thursday and Good Friday. These prayers and resources for worship may be used by various Protestant denominations. The services are ready-to-use and provide options for use in various situations.

Churches that do not use the three-year Revised Common Lectionary are free each year to pick whichever options fit these holy days in their congregation. Churches that do use the three-year lectionary will find directions for the lectionary years, particularly for Palm/Passion Sunday, which has optional Gospel lessons. For Holy Thursday and Good Friday, the lectionary readings are the same for each of the three years. Yet in this volume there are several options for each of these days, using the common scriptures and those related to the lectionary year's version of the Passion story. Two points might be made here about the lectionary: First, Lectionary Year A focuses on the Gospel of Matthew, Lectionary Year B on Mark, and Lectionary Year C on Luke. Second, Lent of 2007 falls in Lectionary Year C, Lent of 2008 in Lectionary Year A, Lent of 2009 in Lectionary Year B, and so on.

The first chapter contains three options for the Palm section of Sunday's service, one from each Gospel reading. These options are ready-to-use but ideas may be interchanged among the three.

Next come six options for the Passion section of Sunday's service, two for each lectionary year, that is two from each of the synoptic Gospels—Matthew, Mark, and Luke.

The second chapter contains six options for Holy Thursday—including services with Communion, footwashing, anointing, dramas, Tenebrae, and a variety of music. The third chapter contains three options for Good Friday.

Because of the use of the Passion story on Palm Sunday as well as on Holy Thursday and Good Friday, this book provides a wide variety of options throughout Holy Week. And as Holy Saturday is part of this week, any of the resources from Passion, Holy Thursday, or Good Friday are appropriate for meditation and prayer on that day.

At the end of the book are definitions that may be shared with your congregation, particularly people who are new Christians, and resources for finding the music mentioned or for further reading.

Because of the high drama of this week and its deep meaning for Christians, we are both pulled toward this week of services and pushed away. Facing the death of Jesus Christ, our own death and sinfulness, and our tendencies to not follow as closely as we should can be difficult. Many congregations are tempted to jump from the celebration of Palm Sunday right to Easter. But there is no way to resurrection except through the cross, for Jesus and for us. One of the reasons Palm and Passion Sunday are together is that the life and death of Jesus are of one piece—his living, healings, feedings, and teachings led in many ways to his death. This can be hard to understand or to try to explain. But what Holy Week does for us is to give us an opportunity to walk beside Jesus, going where he went, experiencing him as a companion and guide for these days and for our lives.

So approach the planning of Holy Week and of these services reverently, in thanksgiving for this amazing gift of our Creator to us—the life, death, and resurrection of Jesus Christ—that by the power of the Holy Spirit we might walk in the ways of God with the companionship of Jesus Christ through all the heights and depths of our lives.

In this book, as in many other worship books, the words in prayers, shown in bold print, are meant to be said in unison, by the whole congregation. Words in regular print are meant to be said by one person: the presider, pastor, or worship leader. Directions are occasionally given in italic print. Scripture quotations are taken from the New Revised Standard Version of the Bible. All prayers and dramas may be reproduced, provided the following credit line and copyright notice appear on each copy: "From *Palm Sunday and Holy Week Services* by Robin Knowles Wallace. Copyright 2006 by Abingdon Press. Reproduced by permission."

CHAPTER ONE

PALM/PASSION SUNDAY

T his Sunday celebrates the triumphal entry of Jesus into the city of Jerusalem, when people waved palm branches and hailed him as a leader come from God. Yet it also commemorates Jesus' passion that occurred later in the week—betrayal and trials, condemnation and crucifixion. This Sunday holds in tension triumph and desolation, glory and rejection. Visuals include palm branches, banners, cloaks, a jar symbolizing the oil of anointing, the cross, purple paraments.

"PALM" SECTION OF SERVICE

1. SUGGESTION FOR PROCESSION, USING THE GOSPEL OF MATTHEW (LECTIONARY YEAR A: 2008, 2011, 2014, 2017)

Processions have been an important part of religion throughout the ages. In the Hebrew Bible Abraham followed God's command to move, and Moses led the Israelites to the Promised Land. People followed Jesus around Galilee and into Jerusalem.

Pilgrimages were an important part of Christianity in the early years and Middle Ages. Today, processions begin many of our worship services, demonstrating our willingness to follow God's call in our lives.

The celebration of Palm Sunday can be one of the most important processions of the church year. This is the culmination of Jesus' followers' celebration of his many healings and feedings, his teachings and care for them. From following Jesus around the small towns and villages of Galilee, people are now willing to follow him into the capital city of Jerusalem, ready to make him king and claim him as Messiah, God's anointed one.

Your Palm Sunday procession may take place within the sanctuary, beginning in the narthex and continuing in and around the sanctuary space. Another way is to gather up persons from Sunday school classes or fellowship time and process into the sanctuary together. Some congregations who are trying to connect with their neighborhood might take the procession out of the church building and into the neighborhood, and then come back to the sanctuary.

For a more formal procession on Palm Sunday, a cross would go first, followed by acolytes, clergy, and people. A less formal procession might begin with something representing the colt or donkey ridden by Jesus. Singing or chanting might be taught to a small group beforehand. At most, have a single half-sheet with words for persons who will participate; anything more is too much for moving and waving palm branches. Have palm branches ready to pass out to persons on the way. Children and youth (or avid sports fans) can be good persons to lead the procession enthusiastically.

Order of Service

Call to Worship (based on Psalm 118:19, 29)

The procession may begin with a call to worship, by the person leading the procession, such as this:
    Open to us the gates of righteousness,
    **That we may enter through them
    and give thanks to the Lord.**

O give thanks to the Lord, for he is good;
God's steadfast love endures forever!

Hymn Suggestions

As the procession gathers, you may sing a hymn for Palm Sunday, such as the following, or another song of praise.

- "All glory, laud and honor" by Theodulph of Orleans, translated John Mason Neale (*Congregation on refrain, choir on verse*)
- "Blessing and praise/Benedictus qui venit" from Taizé
- "Blessed is he who comes in God's name" by John Thornburg
- "Blessed is the one" by Dan Damon (*refrain is the Benedictus used in the Communion service*)
- "Filled with excitement/Mantos y palmas" by Rubén Ruiz Avila, translated Gertrude C. Suppe (*Teach congregation the "Hosanna to the King" section and have choir or children sing the rest*)
- "Crown as your king the king who came crownless" by Thomas H. Troeger
- "He is exalted" by Twila Paris
- "Hosanna, loud hosanna" by Jeanette Threlfall
- "Hosanna! Hosanna!" by Cathy Townley
- "Jesu, Jesu, Hallelujah!" by Thomas H. Troeger
- "King of kings" by Sophie Conty and Naomi Batya
- "Pave the way" by Bret Hesla
- "Tell me the stories of Jesus" by William H. Parker (*stanza 3 "Into the city, I'd follow"*)
- "The rocks would shout if we kept still" by Thomas H. Troeger

Chanting

Chanting is also appropriate and sometimes easier than singing when on the move without instruments.

- Use words of Scripture, such as these from Matthew 21:9, arranged responsively:
  Blessed is the one who comes
  in the name of the Lord!

Hosanna to the Son of David!
Blessed is the one who comes
in the name of the Lord!
Hosanna in the highest heaven!
• Or let the youth of the church write a brief rap that can
involve the congregation with simple phrases of praise.
• Or use the first stanza/refrain of "The rocks would shout if
we kept still" by Thomas H. Troeger

Entering the Sanctuary

*As the procession grows, those at the front will not always be in sync
singing or chanting with those in the back. That is the joy of processions, a multitude of persons, praising God, together in movement and
aim, but all going at their own pace!*

*When you enter the sanctuary, persons may take their places and
either sing a hymn from the list above (if you have chanted) or if you
have sung, then:*
Blessed is the one who comes
in the name of the Lord!
Hosanna to the Son of David!
Blessed is the one who comes
in the name of the Lord!
Hosanna in the highest heaven!

Scripture Reading: Matthew 21:1-11

Prayer

Thank you, our God, for calling us to follow you,
just as Jesus called the disciples long ago.
Thank you for your many blessings to us.
Keep us close to you in this week that begins in triumph
but contains the horrible death of Jesus
whom we love.
Help us hold blessing and passion together in tension
in worship and in our lives.
Through your Holy Spirit we pray. Amen.

Hymn of Transition to Passion Section of Service: "O Christ, what can it mean for us" by Delores Dufner

2. PHILIPPIANS SCRIPTURE AS THE INTERSECTION OF PALM AND PASSION SECTIONS, LEADS IN TO MARK SERVICE (LECTIONARY YEAR B: 2009, 2012, 2015, 2018)

Order of Service

Call to Worship: Psalm 118:1-2

O give thanks to the Lord, for God is good;
God's steadfast love endures forever!
Let all creation say,
"God's steadfast love endures forever."

Hymn: "All praise to thee, for thou, O King divine" by F. Bland Tucker

Scripture Reading: Philippians 2:5-11

Scripture Reflection

Think of yourselves the way Christ Jesus
    thought of himself.
You have been made in the image of God.
Yet, follow the example of Jesus—
look, he didn't boast about how great he was
    or tell a big success story about himself.

5

Instead, he accepted the limitations of a human body,
    not like a superstar,
but like a lowly migrant, traveling the countryside,
    helping whomever he ran into.
This is what got him into trouble,
    upsetting the status quo.
This is what led him to the cross.
Instead of getting cheered into Jerusalem day after day,
Jesus suffered a degrading trial and physical pain,
an embarrassing procession carrying a cross
    through the city and a violent death.
On Easter and everyday since,
    God has had the final word,
taking the death of Jesus and turning it
    into a passage for all of humanity
    into God's love and forgiveness.
For Jesus' willingness to be emptied out in life
    and in death,
God filled everything he did.
Think of yourselves this way—
empty yourself of all that is less than God,
that God may live in you and use your life,
filling you with glory reflected from Christ Jesus.

Silence

Prayer

Gracious God, give us the mind that was in Christ Jesus,
willing to empty ourselves so that you may have
    room to dwell in us.
Draw us closer this week into the mind of Jesus,
that we may understand more deeply his life
    and death and love for us.
Through the Holy Spirit we pray. Amen.

Hymn Suggestions

- "Christ Jesus the lowly" by Ruth C. Duck
- "Crown as your king the king who came crownless" by Thomas H. Troeger
- "Eternal Christ, you rule" by Dan Damon
- "Jesu, Jesu, Hallelujah!" by Thomas H. Troeger
- "Jesus, name above all names" by Naida Hearn
- "Morning glory, starlit sky" by W. H. Vanstone
- "O Christ, what can it mean for us" by Delores Dufner (*connects Palm and Passion*)
- "O lowly Lamb of God most high" by Delores Dufner

3. YOUTH OR CHILDREN'S DRAMA, USING THE GOSPEL OF LUKE (LECTIONARY YEAR C: 2007, 2010, 2013, 2016)

Order of Service

Call to Worship (based on Psalm 118:24, 26)

This is the day that the Lord has made;
Let us rejoice and be glad in it.
Blessed is the one who comes in the name of the Lord.
We bless you from the house of the Lord.

Drama (based on Luke 19:28b-40)

<u>Characters</u>: *Narrator, Jesus, 2–12 Disciples, 1–3 Colt Owners, Crowd, 2 or more Pharisees*
<u>Props</u>: *colt (or played by person), reins, many cloaks, palm branches, placards reading "Bethpage," "Bethany," and "This Way to Jerusalem." Use costumes if desired or set in modern time.*

7

<u>Set Up</u>: *Designate midpoint in sanctuary as the villages of Bethpage and Bethany; colt and its owners are there at beginning of drama and owners may join the crowds after their lines. Narrator is at lectern. Jesus and disciples are at back entrance to sanctuary. Crowds are along the main aisle of sanctuary, from midpoint to front; if enough persons are involved, they may also line the side aisles for a longer procession; these persons may be sitting along the aisle, ready to join in. Practice the procession so Pharisees know where to be—near Jesus when it's time for their lines. If they need to catch up with Jesus, that's fine. Words to be spoken by congregation should be printed in bulletin. Brief prelude to drama might be "Tell me the stories of Jesus" by William H. Parker (stanza 3: "Into the city, I'd follow . . .").*

(As the drama begins, Jesus leads the disciples in from back of sanctuary, stopping one-quarter of way into sanctuary as the narrator ends the first speech.)

> Narrator: Jesus went on ahead, going up to Jerusalem. They came to the Mount of Olives.
>
> Jesus: Go into the village ahead of you. There you will find a colt that has never been ridden. Untie it and bring it to me. If anyone asks, "Why are you untying it?" just say, "The Lord needs it."

(Two or three disciples go to village and begin to untie colt.)

> Colt Owners: Why are you untying our colt?
> Disciples: The Lord needs it.

(Owners shrug to indicate acceptance. Disciples take the colt to Jesus, throw several cloaks on it, and set Jesus on it.)

> Narrator: As Jesus rode along, people kept spreading their cloaks on the road. *(Crowd quietly places cloaks on path.)* As he began going down from the Mount of Olives, the disciples and the followers of Jesus began to praise God joyfully, with loud voices for all the amazing things that they had seen, saying . . .

8

Few Disciples: Blessed is the king who comes in the name of
the Lord!
Some Crowd: Peace in heaven, and glory in the highest
heaven!

*(Each repetition gets louder and procession continues, to front and
then around the sanctuary.)*

All Disciples: Blessed is the king who comes in the name of
the Lord!
All Crowd: Peace in heaven, and glory in the highest
heaven! Blessed is the king who comes in the
name of the Lord!
All Disciples: *(Invite congregation to join in)* Peace in heaven,
and glory in the highest heaven!
All Disciples: Blessed is the king who comes in the name of
the Lord!
Everyone: Peace in heaven and glory in the highest heaven!

*(Procession stops when Pharisees begin speaking. Disciples keep chant
going, but quieter, almost a mutter, through Pharisees' and Jesus' lines.)*

Pharisees: *(Shouting)* Wait! Silence! Teacher, order your
disciples to stop.
Jesus: I tell you, if these people were silent, the stones
would shout out.
Few Disciples: *(Louder)* Blessed is the king who comes in the
name of the Lord!

*(Procession begins again, traveling so that Jesus is at front of sanctu-
ary by the end of the drama. Crowds and disciples begin waving palm
branches. Each repetition gets louder.)*

Some Crowd: Peace in heaven, and glory in the highest
heaven!
All Disciples: Blessed is the king who comes in the name of
the Lord!
All Crowd: Peace in heaven, and glory in the highest
heaven! Blessed is the king who comes in the
name of the Lord!

All Disciples: *(Invite congregation to join in)* Peace in heaven, and glory in the highest heaven!

All Disciples: Blessed is the king who comes in the name of the Lord!

Everyone: Peace in heaven and glory in the highest heaven! Blessed is Jesus, who comes in the name of God! Blessed is Jesus, who comes in the name of God! Hosanna!

Hymn Suggestions

- "A cheering, chanting, dizzy crowd" by Thomas H. Troeger
- "All glory, laud and honor" by Theodulph of Orleans, translated John Mason Neale
- "Crown as your king the king who came crownless" by Thomas H. Troeger
- "Jesu, Jesu, Hallelujah!" by Thomas H. Troeger
- "O Christ, what can it mean for us" by Delores Dufner
- "The rocks would shout if we kept still" by Thomas H. Troeger

Responsive Prayer

Blessed is Jesus, who comes in the name of God.
We praise you, Christ Jesus,
for your amazing acts in our lives.
Yet, like your followers of old,
we turn all too quickly from praise to denial
of your place in our lives.
Stay with us, Lord Jesus, that we may
walk with you into your Passion, the
pouring out of your love for us.
We pray in your name, Father, Son, and Holy Spirit, One God.
Amen.

Hymn of Transition to Passion Section of Service: "O Christ, what can it mean for us" by Delores Dufner

"PASSION" SECTION OF SERVICE

1. MATTHEW'S GOSPEL (LECTIONARY YEAR A)

a. Service of the Passion, as Told in the Gospel of Matthew

Hymn Suggestions

- "I will take some time to pray" by John Thornburg
- "We sang our glad hosannas" by Mary Nelson Keithahn (*stanzas 1–4*)
- "While the courts and priests conspire" by Thomas H. Troeger (*hymn or litany, with its response "Not my will but yours be done."*)

Scripture Reading: Matthew 27:11-26

Prayer

God in pain, Jesus on trial,
You watched and you suffered,
    and so you know our pains and sufferings:
Open our hearts to understand
    the depths of your love for humanity
that we may draw closer to you
    and love you all the more.
We ask this through the power of the Holy Spirit
    that binds us to you. Amen.

Hymn: "Were you there" (these three verses only):

Were you there when they crucified my Lord?
Were you there when they nailed him to the tree?
Were you there when the sun refused to shine?

Scripture Reading: Matthew 27:45-54

Hymn: "O the Lamb," American camp meeting song

Prayer

Crucified Jesus,
with the centurion we proclaim
   that you are the Son of God:
Strengthen our faith, deepen it, and stretch it,
that we may live and proclaim your love
   throughout the world.
We ask this in your holy name. Amen.

Sermon

Offering

Hymn Suggestions

- "What wondrous love is this" U. S. folk hymn
- "When I survey the wondrous cross" by Isaac Watts

Dismissal and Blessing

Go forth, walking closely with Jesus this solemn week.
Know that his love reaches from that faraway time
   into our lives, and blesses us each day.
In the name of the Holy Trinity, go in peace.

b. Voices from the Passion Story, as Told in Matthew 26:14–27:66

<u>Characters</u>: *Judas, Pilate, Pilate's wife, Peter, James, John, 2 Servant Girls, Bystander, 2 Owners of Palm Sunday colt, 2 Owners of the Upper Room, Centurion, 4 Voices*

These readings may be used together, in the order given, or individually. They may be read from the lectern or from stations throughout the sanctuary.

Judas

I was one of the twelve; we left our jobs and followed Jesus around the countryside for almost three years. The day of the palms, that triumphal entry, that should have been the beginning of wonderful things. Jesus could have taken over that city, but he just went around the next several days doing the same things he had always done—teaching, healing, eating with outcasts.

So I tried to force his hand. I went to the chief priests and said, "What will you give me if I betray him to you?" They gave me thirty pieces of silver and I began to look for the right time to start things moving.

Jesus himself gave me the clue that the time was right on Thursday night, as while we were eating, he said, "Truly I tell you, one of you will betray me." He looked right at me and I thought he understood. But he was also telling us something about the bread and his body and the cup and his blood—it was too confusing, so I left and got the chief priests to come to the garden where we went sometimes for prayer.

The chief priests brought along a mob; I think they were afraid of Jesus' power. As I went up to Jesus, I greeted him with love and yet with fear—would it turn out alright? "Greetings, Teacher!" He said, "Friend, do what you are here to do." Then the crowd came and laid hands on Jesus and arrested him.

But the next twenty-four hours didn't go like they were supposed to. Jesus got very quiet and instead of smiting the rulers and taking power, he was condemned. No, no, how could I have gotten it so wrong! Now Jesus was condemned to die, like a common criminal, on a cross. I took the money, ran back to the priests and said, "I have sinned by betraying innocent blood." They could not have cared less; they were happy to see Jesus out of their way. I threw the money at them and went off to do the only thing I could think of; I died before he did.

Pilate and his Wife (with Peter, James and John, Servant Girls 1 and 2, and Bystander)

Pilate: Being governor is supposed to be a good position, but not out here, dealing with petty arguments between people day in and day out. Then they bring someone to me who seems innocent, so I know something political or religiously political is going on. To keep the people happy I always release a prisoner on their festival— this seems like a no-brainer, Barabbas or this one called the Messiah.

Pilate's Wife: But I had a dream, chaos and confusion, I hardly slept last night at all. I don't know what's going on in your day, husband. Still, I hear the rumblings outside our home and suddenly it seems important that you not have anything to do with this man. Please, be careful.

Pilate: We'll talk later, my dear. For now, the crowd is restless, it seems, for blood. So I will symbolically wash my hands of this affair, since it seems to be rushing ahead of its own accord.

Peter: *(with James and John)* I wanted to stand by Jesus forever. Teachings, healings, and followers . . . he was everything I needed in my life. I told him at our last meal, "I will never desert you."

James: So did we all. But then the three of us couldn't even stay awake while Jesus prayed in Gethsemane.

John: We were so tired—traveling, the excitement of entering into Jerusalem, and then all the excitement of the city at Passover—I tried to stay awake . . .

James: But we were pathetic. Three times Jesus caught us with our eyes closed.

Peter: I wanted to tell Jesus I was just resting and thinking over what he said at dinner, but the truth was I fell asleep.

(Servant Girls 1 and 2 and Bystander, from another part of the sanctuary)

Servant Girl 1: You can tell me you weren't with that Jesus the Galilean, mister, but I know I saw you.

Servant Girl 2: You told me you didn't know Jesus of Nazareth, but you looked embarrassed and like a liar to me.

Bystander: Your accent gave you away, man. You're one of that guy's followers.

Peter: *(with sadness)* I couldn't stay awake even when Jesus asked me to. I swore I didn't know him— not just once or twice, but three times. How could I have done this? What kind of follower am I?

Owners of the Palm Sunday Colt and the Upper Room (U.R.)

Colt Owner 1: We kept our colt tied up on the edge of the village.

Colt Owner 2: On the first day of the week two strangers came and started untying our colt.

Colt Owner 1: I asked them, "What are you doing?"

Colt Owner 2: They said, "The Lord has need of it."

Colt Owner 1: I dreamed the night before that someone took our colt to ride it into Jerusalem.

Colt Owner 2: So what could we say but, "Take the colt and take good care of it"?

U.R. Owner 1: Ah, that sounds like what happened to us on Thursday morning.

U.R. Owner 2: Two strangers showed up at our home and said they were sent from the Teacher.

U.R. Owner 1: They said, "The time is near. The Teacher will keep Passover at your house with his disciples."

U.R. Owner 2: What could we do? We said, "The room upstairs is clean. Use it as you will."

U.R. Owner 1: And now it is Saturday and the city seems deathly quiet.

Colt Owner 1: Someone told me that the King of the Jews was crucified yesterday.

U.R. Owner 2: Who was that? How could those people have a king?

Colt Owner 2: I heard he was a teacher who traveled up from Galilee, who healed Samuel's cousin.

U.R. Owner 1: Who knows? He's dead now.

The Centurion

"This is Jesus, the King of the Jews," were the words we nailed above his head. Then crowds and religious leaders came by and taunted him about being the Son of God and saving himself. There seemed to be more of a crowd than we usually get; ordinarily it's just the crime victim's family and neighbors. This man seemed to have made many people angry, yet there was a group of women on the edges, weeping. And he never talked back to his tormentors, not like some, who curse the world as they die. We watched him, holding on to the little bit of human dignity he could muster—dying, quietly dying. But as he gave up life, he cried out with a loud voice to God, the earth shook, and I saw a look in his eyes as they closed . . . I think it must be true, that this man was God's Son.

Those Who Had Been Dead

Voice 1: Whatever it is like to be dead, we were.
Followers of Jesus,

Voice 2: believers in his miracles,

Voice 3: disciples of his teachings,

Voice 4: lovers of God, we had died of old age or circum-
stance, before Jesus did.

Voice 1: But, suddenly it was like waking up from a pow-
erful dream:

Voice 2: we heard his voice crying out,

Voice 3: the earth shook,

Voice 4: rocks split into pieces,

All: and our tombs opened up.

Voice 1: We started and then lay there, still.

Voice 2: *(Pause)* Later, when he rose on the third day,
we went into the city,

Voice 3: singly and by twos,

Voice 4: appearing to those we had loved and left
behind.

Voice 1: They told us the amazing news of Jesus' resurrection,

All: and in seeing us, they believed it was true.

Hymn Suggestions

- "Crown as your king the king who came crownless" by Thomas H. Troeger
- "Crucified Savior" by Thomas H. Troeger
- "Eternal Christ, you rule" by Dan Damon
- "Eternal Christ, you rule" by Dan Damon
- "I will take some time to pray" by John Thornburg
- "Kneeling in the garden grass" by Thomas H. Troeger (*hymn or litany, with its response* "Not my will but yours be done.")
- "The child is sleeping sound" *[about Judas]* by Shirley Erena Murray

Optional Meditation: "The cross on the hill is the measuring rod" poem by Thomas H. Troeger

2. MARK'S GOSPEL (LECTIONARY YEAR B)

a. Anointing of Jesus' Feet and Its Place in the Passion Story

Hymn Suggestions

The first four hymns for this Scripture leave the woman unnamed; the second two name her Mary as in John 12:1-8.
- "An unexpected guest arrived" by John Thornburg
- "A prophet-woman broke a jar" by Brian Wren (*especially stanza 1*)
- "Woman in the night" by Brian Wren (*stanza 4, "Woman at the feast"*)
- "With my whole heart" by Shirley Erena Murray
- "Said Judas to Mary" by Sidney Carter
- "When Mary bathed our savior's feet" by Ruth C. Duck

Scripture Presentation: Mark 14:3-9

<u>Characters</u>: *Narrator, Jesus, 2 or more Voices, Woman. (Narrator's voice should be strong; Voices 1 & 2 are commenting on the Narrator's text.)*

Narrator and Jesus sit at table placed in center of the chancel area. Voices (2 or more) come from either side. Woman with elegant jar of ointment is the primary actor and mover.

Narrator: While Jesus was at Bethany . . .
  Voice 1: a town on the Mount of Olives,
  Voice 2: where Lazarus, Martha and Mary lived,
Narrator: at the house of Simon the leper . . .
  Voice 1: Was he the leper cured by Jesus in the first chapter of Mark?
  Voice 2: You mean the one who couldn't keep quiet about his healing?
Narrator: as Jesus sat at the table . . .

Voice 1: a guest at Simon's feast,
Voice 2: the Tuesday after Palm Sunday,
Narrator: a woman came in with an alabaster jar of very costly ointment of nard. (*Woman enters.*)
Voice 1: The writer of Mark doesn't tell us her name.
Voice 2: It must have been a beautiful jar, made of white stone.
Voice 1: Nard was a fragrant ointment made from a plant that might have had healing properties.
Voice 2: It's one of the ointments used when people were buried in Jesus' time.
Narrator: The woman broke open the jar and poured the ointment on Jesus' head. (*Woman acts.*)
Voice 1: Prophets were anointed like this in the Hebrew Bible.
Voice 2: So were priests and kings, even King David.
Voice 1: The anointing marked people as set apart and holy.
Voice 2: *Messiah* and *Christ* mean "the Anointed One."
Voice 1: So this woman acted like Samuel to Saul and David.
Voice 2: Then, she was God's prophet.
Narrator: But some people said angrily,
Voice 1: What a waste!
Voice 2: Why did Jesus let her do that?
Voice 1: That stuff was worth a year's income.
Voice 2: She could have given that money to the poor.
Voice 1: (*to woman*) Hey, you!
Voice 2: Stop!
Jesus: Let her alone! Why are you bothering her? She has been kind to me. There will always be those in need, because people have not shared. You can be kind to the poor everyday, and I hope you will. But I won't always be with you in this body. (*Turns to the woman*) Thank you for this anointing. You have honored me and prepared my body for its burial.

Prayer

Anointed Lord,
We give you thanks for this woman
  and her act of honoring you.
Teach us so to follow her example
  that your name and your deeds will be glorified.
In your name we pray. Amen.

Hymn Suggestions

- "Christ, whose glory fills the skies" by Charles Wesley
- "Glory be to the Father" traditional
- "In my life, Lord, be glorified" by Bob Kilpatrick
- "My tribute: To God be the glory" by Andraé Crouch

b. General Passion from Mark and Philippians, Includes Congregation in Scripture Reading

This section of the Palm/Passion service may either follow one of the Passion options above or it may stand alone as a Holy Thursday or Good Friday service. The story of Jesus' passion, as told in the Gospel of Mark is framed by Philippians 2:5-11, one of the hymns of the early church. The Scripture reading from Mark calls for a large list of characters and may either be read by a practiced cast or by the congregation who have received a part when they entered the sanctuary that day. There are enough crowd parts for even large congregations to all take part.

Hymn Suggestions

- "All praise to thee, for thou, O King divine" by F. Bland Tucker
- "Ask ye what great thing I know" by Johann C. Schwedler
- "At the name of Jesus" by Caroline M. Noel
- "Canticle of Christ's obedience" found in *The United Methodist Hymnal* #167

- "Hallelujah! What a Savior" by Philip P. Bliss
- "Lift high the cross" by George William Kitchin and Michael Robert Newbolt

Scripture Reading: Philippians 2:5-11

Prayer

Let the same mind be in you
   that was in Christ Jesus.
Let us pray:
You made us in your image, O God,
   but we know we are not you.
Give us the mind that was in Christ Jesus,
   that we may become more obedient,
   emptied of self, and full of you.
And we will proclaim with our lives
   that Jesus Christ is Lord,
to your glory, Holy Trinity, one God,
   now and forever. Amen.

Hymn Suggestions

- "Kneeling in the garden grass" and "While the courts and priests conspire" by Thomas H. Troeger (*hymn or litany, with shared response "Not my will but yours be done."*)
- "Crown as your king the king who came crownless" by Thomas H. Troeger
- "Jesus saw the path to death" by Dan Damon
- "Acclamations for the Passion" by Delores Dufner, using Mark version (*sung after each section of the reading, when narrators change*)
- "This is the mind-set of one who has come" by Shirley Erena Murray

Optional Meditation: "The cross on the hill is the measuring rod" poem by Thomas H. Troeger

Scripture Reading (adapted from Mark 14:32-42, 15:1-39)

<u>Individual Characters</u>: 4 Narrators, Jesus, Pilate, Reader, Wine-bearer, Centurion
<u>Groups</u>: Crowd, Soldiers, Deriders, Chief Priests & Scribes, Bystanders.
If done as a drama, add a group of Disciples who move but have no lines.
<u>Prop:</u> Placard reading "The King of the Jews".

SCENE I

Narrator 1: Jesus and his disciples went to a place called Gethsemane; and he said to the disciples,

Jesus: Sit here while I pray.

Narrator 1: He took with him Peter and James and John, and began to be distressed and agitated. And he said to them,

Jesus: I am deeply grieved, even to death; remain here, and keep awake.

Narrator 1: And going a little farther, Jesus threw himself on the ground and prayed that, if it were possible, the hour might pass from him. He said,

Jesus: *Abba*, Father, for you all things are possible; remove this cup from me; yet, not what I want, but what you want.

Narrator 1: He came and found the disciples sleeping; and he said to Peter,

Jesus: Simon, are you asleep? Could you not stay awake one hour? Keep awake and pray that you may not come into the time of trial; the spirit indeed is willing, but the flesh is weak.

Narrator 1: And again Jesus went away and prayed, saying the same words.

Jesus: *Abba*, Father, for you all things are possible; remove this cup from me; yet, not what I want, but what you want.

Narrator 1: And once more Jesus came and found the disciples sleeping, for their eyes were very heavy; and they did not know what to say to him.

Jesus: *Abba*, Father, for you all things are possible; remove this cup from me; yet, not what I want, but what you want.

Narrator 1: Jesus came a third time and said to them,

Jesus: Are you still sleeping and taking your rest? Enough! The hour has come; the Son of Man is betrayed into the hands of sinners. Get up; let us be going. See, my betrayer is at hand.

SCENE II

Narrator 2: As soon as it was morning, the chief priests held a consultation with the elders and scribes and the whole council. They bound Jesus, led him away, and handed him over to Pilate. Pilate asked Jesus,

Pilate: Are you the King of the Jews?

Jesus: You say so.

Narrator 2: Then the chief priests accused him of many things. Pilate asked Jesus again,

Pilate: Have you no answer? See how many charges they bring against you.

Narrator 2: But Jesus made no further reply, so that Pilate was amazed.

Now at the festival Pilate used to release a prisoner for them, anyone for whom they asked. A man called Barabbas was in prison with the rebels who had committed murder during the insurrection. So the crowd came and began to ask Pilate to do for them according to his custom. Then Pilate answered the crowd,

Pilate: Do you want me to release for you the King of the Jews?

Narrator 2: Pilate realized that it was out of jealousy that the chief priests had handed Jesus over. But the chief priests stirred up the crowd to have him

release Barabbas for them instead. Pilate spoke
to the crowd again,

Pilate: Then what do you wish me to do with the man
you call the King of the Jews?

Crowd: Crucify him!

Pilate: Why? What evil has he done?

Crowd: Crucify him!

Narrator 2: So Pilate, wishing to satisfy the crowd, released
Barabbas for them; and after flogging Jesus, he
handed him over to be crucified.

SCENE III

Narrator 3: Then the soldiers led Jesus into the courtyard of
the palace (that is, the governor's headquar-
ters); and they called together the whole court.
And they clothed Jesus in a purple cloak, and
after twisting some thorns into a crown, they
put it on him. And the soldiers began saluting
him,

Soldiers: Hail, King of the Jews!

Narrator 3: They struck his head with a reed, spat upon
him, and knelt down in homage to him.

Soldiers: Hail, King of the Jews!

Narrator 3: After mocking him, they stripped him of the
purple cloak and put his own clothes on him.
Then they led him out to crucify him.

SCENE IV

Narrator 4: The soldiers compelled a passerby, who was
coming in from the country, to carry Jesus'
cross. It was Simon of Cyrene, the father of
Alexander and Rufus. Then they brought Jesus
to the place called Golgotha (which means the
place of a skull). And they offered him wine
mixed with myrrh, but he did not take it. And
they crucified Jesus, and divided his clothes
among them, casting lots to decide what each
should take.

SCENE V

Narrator 1: It was nine o'clock in the morning when they crucified him. The inscription of the charge against him read,

Reader: "The King of the Jews."

Narrator 1: And with Jesus they crucified two bandits, one on his right and one on his left. Those who passed by derided him, shaking their heads and saying,

Deriders: Aha! You who would destroy the temple and build it in three days, save yourself, and come down from the cross!

Narrator 2: In the same way the chief priests, along with the scribes, were also mocking him among themselves and saying,

Priests/Scribes: He saved others; he cannot save himself. Let the Messiah, the King of Israel, come down from the cross now, so that we may see and believe.

Narrator 2: Those who were crucified with him also taunted him.

Narrator 3: When it was noon, darkness came over the whole land until three in the afternoon. At three o'clock Jesus cried out with a loud voice,

Jesus: My God, my God, why have you forsaken me?

Narrator 3: When some of the bystanders heard it, they said,

Bystanders: Listen, he is calling for Elijah.

Narrator 4: And someone ran, filled a sponge with sour wine, put it on a stick, and gave it to him to drink, saying,

Winebearer: Wait, let us see whether Elijah will come to take him down.

Narrator 4: Then Jesus gave a loud cry and breathed his last.

Narrator 1: And the curtain of the temple was torn in two, from top to bottom.

Narrator 2: Now when the centurion, who stood facing
him, saw that in this way Jesus breathed his last,
he said,

Centurion: Truly this man was God's Son!

(Silence and stillness for at least fifteen seconds, up to three minutes for meditation)

Narrator 3: There were also women looking on the crucifixion from a distance; among them were Mary
Magdalene, and Mary the mother of James the
younger and of Joses, and Salome. These women
used to follow Jesus and provided for him when
he was in Galilee; and there were many other
women who had come up with him to Jerusalem.

A Statement of Faith (based on Philippians 2:9-11)

Like those women, standing faithfully at the cross,
 we have observed your passion, Lord Jesus Christ.
This is the great thing we know:
 Jesus Christ, the crucified.
This is what we proclaim:
Through the faithfulness of Jesus Christ,
 who was equally and utterly divine and human,
 God has been highly exalted.
What looked to be death for Jesus
 and defeat for his disciples
 is not the end of the story.
God is not finished with us yet.
The Holy Spirit is alive and working in our world.
Through that same Spirit we confess
 that Jesus Christ is Lord,
 to the glory of God our Creator. Amen.

Benediction

Go now in the name of Jesus Christ, the crucified. Tell the world
with your mouths and your lives that God so loved the world that

God was willing to die for us. May the blessing of the One who made us, the One who faced death for us, and the One who sustains our lives, the Holy Trinity, be with us all, now and forever more. Amen.

3. LUKE'S GOSPEL (LECTIONARY YEAR C)

a. Last Supper and Disciples' Discussion about Who Is Greatest (Includes Children's Sermon)

Who Is the Greatest? Drama (based on Luke 22:14, 21-27)

<u>Characters</u>: *Narrator (at lectern), 12 Disciples, and Jesus (all eating at table)*

Narrator: When the time was right, Jesus and the disciples ate a meal together, a meal which turned out to be Jesus' last meal on earth before he died.

Jesus: What is coming, is coming. But one of you will help it come, by turning me over to the authorities.

Disciple 1: *(to neighbor)* Who do you think it is?

Disciple 2: Not one of us!

Disciple 3: *(to neighbor)* One of us can't be trusted.

Disciple 4: Surely the authorities know Jesus and who he is.

Disciple 5: *(seated at the end; turns to congregation and away from table)* How did Jesus find out? Does he know it's me?

(Silence for at least one minute, while eating continues.)

Disciple 6: Well, whoever turns Jesus in, that person won't be the greatest of us.

Disciple 7: The greatest of us . . . wouldn't that be John?

Disciple 8: No, I think it would be Simon Peter, he's a stronger leader.

Disciple 9: But John is kind.

Disciple 10: But others are older; they should be the greatest, the first after Jesus.

Disciple 11: I think I should be next after Jesus.

Disciple 12: Are you kidding?

Disciple 1: Who's strongest?

Disciple 2: Who's smartest?

Disciple 3: Who's the best leader?

Disciples 4-6: (*together*) Who's the greatest?

(*Silence for fifteen seconds.*)

Jesus: Haven't I taught you anything? The greatest among you must be the one who serves. You cannot name "greatest" like the world does; you must be different. Who serves others? Who is humble? Who lives a faithful life without showing off? Strive for these things. Try to be more like I have tried to show you—different from what you see in the world. Be those who serve; who love.

Children's Sermon (to follow the drama)

What were the disciples doing? Why did they argue? Have you ever seen people fight about who gets to be the boss? What did Jesus say about that? (*Help them understand and voice that we are not called to be the boss, but to love and serve.*) How can you help serve at home or at our church? (*Be ready to help name some ways children can serve.*)

b. General Passion from Luke with Two Dramas: "Daughters of Jerusalem" and "Father, Forgive Them"

Hymn Suggestions

- "Acclamations for the Passion" by Delores Dufner, using Luke version (*sung after each section of the reading*)

- "Crown as your king the king who came crownless" by Thomas H. Troeger
- "Jesus saw the path to death" by Dan Damon
- "Kneeling in the garden grass" and "While the courts and priests conspire" by Thomas H. Troeger *(hymn or litany, with shared response "Not my will but yours be done.")*
- "We look down deep to look out far" by Thomas H. Troeger

Optional Meditation: "The cross on the hill is the measuring rod" poem by Thomas H. Troeger

Daughters of Jerusalem Drama
(based on Luke 22:54–23:28)

<u>Characters</u>: *Narrator and 3 Women*

Narrator: After a night of trials and abuse at the house of the high priest and after three trials that morning at the council of elders and at the offices of Herod and Pilate, Jesus was taken away to be crucified. He had been yelled at, made fun of, challenged, and beaten. On the way to the place where criminals were crucified, Jesus, weak and sore, could no longer carry the heavy crossbar of his cross. So the authorities grabbed Simon from the town of Cyrene and made him carry the crossbar and walk behind Jesus. People were following Jesus and the two criminals who were also to be crucified. Some were jeering, but some of the women were sobbing with deep grief. The awful procession stopped as Jesus turned to the women and said "Daughters of Jerusalem, do not cry for me. Weep for yourselves and your children. For if they have done this while I am alive, what will they do next?"

Woman #1: I was so sad. There was the one we cheered on Palm Sunday. We thought he might be the Messiah.

Woman #2:   I knew his mother, Mary. To see her son treated like a dangerous criminal . . .

Woman #3:   That man healed my daughter. He seems so good. How could the authorities treat him like this?

Woman #1:   Yet he told us not to cry for him.

Woman #2:   He looked awful, no sleep for two days, beaten, hungry, and exhausted. How could we not cry, we who loved him?

Woman #3:   His words seemed a warning to me . . . to "weep for myself and my children." Will my daughter become ill again when he dies?

Woman #2:   I'm sure she'll stay well. Remember how he said, "Don't cry" before he healed the widow's son and the ruler of the synagogue's daughter? *[See Luke 7:13, 8:52]*

Woman #1:   Then do you think he knows about something that will happen to us?

Woman #2:   Or does he know how sad and depressing this world will be without his healings, his stories, his feedings?

Woman #3:   What if his dying means the end of love and light in the world?

(*Women freeze in place for one minute*)

"Father, Forgive Them," Drama
(based on Luke 23:32-39a, 49)

<u>Characters</u>: *3 Women (who followed Jesus from Galilee, standing at a distance from the cross), 1 Man (a stranger)*

Woman #1:   They are done pounding in the nails. You can look now, sister.

Woman #2:   It breaks my heart. How could this have happened?

Woman #3:   Shhh . . . it looks like his mouth is moving. Sir, did you hear what he said?

Man: It's bizarre. He must have gone crazy from his

ordeal. I think he said "Father, forgive them, for they don't know what they are doing." Is his dad still alive?

Woman #3: "Father, forgive them . . . for they don't know what they are doing." I don't think he means Joseph.

Woman #2: Of course not. Have you forgotten already? He means God.

Woman #3: Then who is "them" and "they"? Who needs to be forgiven?

Woman #1: And how could he think of forgiveness when he's dying, being killed so cruelly?

Woman #2: But it seems in character for Jesus. He talked about forgiveness in the prayer he gave us and in that story about forgiving others more than once. *[See Luke 7:3-4]*

Woman #3: You think he is forgiving the ones who put in the nails?

Woman #1: Or the crowd who shouted "Crucify him" to Pilate?

Woman #2: Or those who put him on trial?

Woman #3: Or those who beat him?

Woman #1: Or Peter who denied him?

Woman #2: Or Judas who turned him over to the authorities?

Woman #3: Or the disciples who fell asleep in the garden while he prayed?

Woman #1: Or us for not speaking up?

Woman #2: Or those of us who forgot to tell him "thank you"?

Woman #3: Or the world for not understanding?

(Silence for fifteen seconds)

All Women: Whatever—whoever—he asked God to forgive us all. We are forgiven!

CHAPTER TWO

HOLY THURSDAY

INTRODUCTION

Holy Thursday begins the most holy three days in the Christian year. In the Jewish manner of accounting days, beginning with sunset, Holy Thursday marks the first day. These twenty-four hours hold a last meal with Jesus' disciples, footwashing, prayer in a garden, betrayal, trials, and denial, all leading to crucifixion. Holy Thursday has traditionally been called *Maundy Thursday*, referring to the new commandment (Latin: *mandatum*) that Jesus gives the disciples, "to love one another" (John 13:31-35). As the church continues to reach out to seekers, using the name *Holy Thursday* may be less confusing.

This is a service of high drama, and it can engage congregations in multisensory ways with: music, drama, movement, prayer, silence, water for footwashing with a pitcher and basin, towels for drying feet, the bread and cup of Communion, purple colors, rough textures, jar of anointing oil, a lamb for Passover and the Lamb of God, and rocks representing the garden of Gethsemane.

Hymn Suggestions

- "A new commandment" anonymous
- "A place at the table" by Shirley Erena Murray

- "An upper room" by Fred Pratt Green
- "Because thou hast said" by Charles Wesley
- "Become to us the living bread" by Miriam Drury
- "Bread of the world in mercy broken" by Reginald Heber
- "Christ, let us come with you" by Shirley Erena Murray
- "Draw us in the Spirit's tether" by Percy Dearmer
- "Let us break bread together" African American spiritual
- "O food to pilgrims given" anonymous, translated by J. A. L. Riley
- "O the depth of love divine" by Charles Wesley
- "Stay with me/Bleibet hier" from Taizé
- "The bread of life for all is broken" by Timothy Tingfang Lew
- "Three holy days enfold us now" by Delores Dufner
- "Live in charity/Ubi caritas" from Taizé
- "What wondrous love is this" U. S. folk hymn
- "When Israel was in Egypt's land" African American spiritual

1. LAST SUPPER AND PASSOVER

The synoptic Gospels (Matthew, Mark, and Luke) place the last meal of Jesus with the disciples as the Passover meal of Jewish tradition. John's Gospel focuses on the death of Jesus at the same time that the lambs were slaughtered for Passover, thus placing the Last Supper as a pre-Passover meal. This service attempts to hold those biblical accounts in tension. There are some churches that try to combine Passover meals with Holy Thursday Communion celebrations. As Christians, we cannot fully step into Jesus' traditions, although we need to try to understand and to respect them. Thus, this service is a proposal not to replicate a Passover meal but to observe what we know as Christians: that God in Jesus took both special and ordinary meals and gave them new meaning, that as we feast at Christ's table we encounter the living God who has died and risen again for our salvation and for the salvation of the whole world.

Introduction

This night is part of a time of remembrance for the Hebrew people. In a time of famine they had gone to the land of Egypt, where Joseph had helped the Egyptians to plan and store food. Now, in the time of Moses, the Hebrew people are in slavery, and God is about to do a mighty act.

Call to Worship: Psalm 116:1-2

I love the Lord, because he has heard
   my voice and my supplications.
Because God inclined an ear to me,
   therefore I will call on him as long as I live.

Hymn: "When Israel was in Egypt's land"
African American spiritual

Scripture Reading: Exodus 12:1-14

Prayer

God of the Hebrew people,
you sent Joseph, Moses, Aaron and Miriam
   to guide your people,
   feeding and freeing them.
Jesus celebrated this yearly remembrance
with his family growing up
   and then as an adult with his disciples.
As we enter into this Passover season,
guide us into the succession of your people
   throughout history
that we might know you as our guardian,
   guide, and liberator all of our days. Amen.

Invitation to the Table:
Passover, Last Supper, and Crucifixion in Dialogue

Three voices and congregational response; leader instructs congregation to respond with "The Lord is our Salvation" when they hear the words ". . . a time of remembrance."

Voice 1: A lamb from sheep or goats,
killed at twilight as the congregation of Israel
assembled in an alien land:
Roasted lamb, unleavened bread,
and bitter herbs.
Dressed for travel, with walking sticks in hand,
eating quickly.
This is a day when the Lord God saw the lamb's
blood on our doorposts and passed over,
sparing our children.
This is a time of remembrance

All: The Lord is our salvation.

Voice 2: *(Read Matthew 26:17-19)*

Voice 3: The synoptic Gospels—Matthew, Mark, and
Luke—tell us that Jesus' last meal with the disciples was the Passover meal:
Roasted lamb, unleavened bread,
and bitter herbs.
Dressed for travel, with walking sticks in hand,
eating quickly.
This is a day when the Lord God saw the lamb's
blood on our doorposts and passed over,
sparing our children.
This is a time of remembrance

All: The Lord is our salvation.

Voice 1: But John's Gospel tells the story slightly differently. Here it is the season of Passover but not
yet time for the meal itself.

Voice 2: *(Read John 13:1, 3-4; 18:28, 19:14)*

Voice 3: Jesus washes the feet of the disciples, is arrested
in the garden, and stands trial through the

night at the homes of Annas and Caiaphas. As morning dawns he is led to Pilate's headquarters.

Voice 1: But the Jewish leaders will not go in here for it is the day of preparation for Passover. To enter Pilate's headquarters would make them unclean. So as the lambs are being prepared for Passover, Jesus is prepared for crucifixion—the Lamb of God.

This is a time of remembrance.

All: The Lord is our salvation.

Voice 2: Passover meal or preparation,

Voice 3: Communion for us is both:

Voice 1: Our Passover into freedom from sin and death—

Voice 2: Meal for the journey, eaten on the go—

Voice 3: And Christ is our Passover lamb,

Voice 1: Whose blood marks all of us and guarantees our safety as God's own.

3 Voices: This is a time of remembrance.

All: The Lord is our salvation.

Agnus Dei/Lamb of God

Tradition words of the Agnus Dei are:

Lamb of God, who takes away the sins of the world, have mercy on us.

Lamb of God, who takes away the sins of the world, have mercy on us.

Lamb of God, who takes away the sins of the world, grant us your peace.

This may also be said or sung responsively, as follows:

Lamb of God, who takes away the sins of the world, **have mercy on us.**

Lamb of God, who takes away the sins of the world, **have mercy on us.**

Lamb of God, who takes away the sins of the world,
grant us your peace.

An alternative version might be:
Jesus Christ, Lamb of God,
have mercy on us.
Jesus Christ, bearer of our sins,
have mercy on us.
Jesus Christ, redeemer of the world,
give us your peace.

Hymn Suggestions

Any of these may be sung during the distribution of Communion (or during the service itself)
- "Because thou hast said" by Charles Wesley
- "Holy God of cloud and flame" by Ruth C. Duck (*could be used as the "Sanctus/Holy, Holy, Holy" during The Great Thanksgiving)*
- "In the singing" by Shirley Erena Murray
- "O lowly Lamb of God most high" by Delores Dufner
- "The bread of life for all is broken" by Timothy Tingfang Lew
- "This holy covenant was made" by Sylvia G. Dunstan
- "Way of all ways" by Dan Damon
- "We look down deep to look out far" by Thomas H. Troeger
- "When from bondage we are summoned" by Delores Dufner

Great Thanksgiving

On this night, we gather as the Hebrew people
gathered in exile
to share the Lamb and celebrate
your passing over them in mercy.
Holy, holy, holy Lord, God of power and might:
Heaven and earth are full of your glory.
Hosanna in the highest!

Blessed is the one who comes in the name of the Lord.
  Hosanna in the highest!
On this night, we pass on to children and strangers
  what we have received from you, Lord Jesus:
Who on the night you left us, took bread
  blessed it, broke it
  and gave it to the disciples, saying,
  "Do this in remembrance of me,"
Then at the table with the disciples
  Jesus took the cup and said,
  "This is my life for you,
  share in its newness and remember me."
And so we remember:
Christ has died, Christ is risen,
  Christ will come again.
As we remember you, Lord Jesus Christ
pour out yourself again for us and on these gifts
  of bread and cup.
By your Holy Spirit make us living remembrances
of your great love and life.
Fill us with a new understanding of love
  among all your children
that others may see our witness
  and draw close to you.
We praise your name, Holy God,
the One who made us,
the One who faced death for us,
and the One who sustains our lives, Holy Trinity. **Amen.**

Hymn: "O food to pilgrims given" anonymous, translated by
J. A. L. Riley

No Benediction—Depart in Silence

2. FOOTWASHING, BASED ON JOHN 13

A traditional text for this night in the Christian year is found in John 13, where Jesus washes the feet of the disciples and gives them a new commandment, "to love one another." It is this commandment of Jesus that gives us the word *Maundy* that comes from the Latin *mandatum*. Footwashing is common in some traditions but not in others, so prepare people before this service if you are opening up this opportunity to other than the characters in the drama.

Directions are given below both for involving only the characters of the drama or others. If you would like to begin such a tradition for the congregation, you might start with it as part of the drama the first year; the second year invite leaders of the congregation who would be willing; the third year, invite the entire congregation, knowing always that some will choose not to participate. Singing during the time of footwashing is a way for those persons who remain seated to participate in a different way. This service might also lead into Communion, using a standard service or one of the Communion services in this volume.

Hymn: *"Live in charity/Ubi caritas"* from Taizé
(sing for three to five minutes)

Opening Prayer

God, who comes in human form and kneels
    to wash our dirty, dusty feet:
We give you thanks for such great kindness
    and mercy toward us.
Open our hearts that we might understand
    your generous love for us
    and then share that love with the world.
We ask this in your holy name. Amen.

Footwashing Drama or Scripture Reading
from John 13:1, 3-10a, 12-15, 17, 33a, 34-35

<u>Characters</u>: Narrator, Simon Peter, Jesus
<u>Props</u>: An outer robe for Jesus, a long towel around his waist, a pitcher
with water, and a basin

    *To wash feet during the drama: The character of Jesus may actually
wash the feet of the character of Simon Peter after Simon Peter gives
his consent during the reading of the drama, as noted.*

    *The following may also be read as Scripture, followed by a time of
footwashing, to demonstrate our willingness to follow Christ in ser-vice
and in love. If opening the footwashing to the congregation or selected
members, prepare folks before the service. Then have several pitchers
and bowls, and separate towels for each person's feet. People getting
their feet washed would hold them over the bowl (rather than in the
bowl), so that water might be poured over their feet and then the feet
wrapped in the towel and dried.*

    Either way, the congregation may sing:

- "An upper room did our Lord prepare" by Fred Pratt Green
  (stanzas 3 and 4)
- "Do you who follow understand?" by Delores Dufner
- "Jesu, Jesu, fill us with your love" by Tom Colvin
- "When Mary bathed our Savior's feet" by Ruth Duck *(begin
  with stanza 2, "Since Jesus knew his time had come")*

Narrator: Now, before the festival of the Passover, Jesus
               knew that his hour had come to depart from
               this world and go to the Father. Having loved
               his own who were in the world, he loved them
               to the end. And during supper, Jesus, knowing
               that he had come from God and was going to
               God, got up from the table, took off his outer
               robe, and tied a towel around himself. (*Jesus, do
               so.*) Then he poured water into a basin and
               began to wash the disciples' feet and to wipe
               them with the towel that was tied around him.
               Jesus came to Simon Peter, who said to him,

Simon Peter: Lord, are you going to wash my feet?

Jesus: You do not know now what I am doing, but later you will understand.

Simon Peter: You will never wash my feet.

Jesus: Unless I wash you, you have no share with me.

Simon Peter: Lord, then not my feet only but also my hands and my head!

Jesus: One who has bathed does not need to wash, except for the feet, but is entirely clean. *(if washing feet as part of the drama, do so here)*

Narrator: After Jesus had washed their feet, put on his robe *(Jesus, do so)*, and returned to the table, he said to the disciples,

Jesus: Do you know what I have done to you? You call me Teacher and Lord—and you are right, for that is what I am. So if I, your Lord and Teacher, have washed your feet, you also ought to wash one another's feet. For I have set you an example that you also should do as I have done to you. If you know these things, you are blessed if you do them.

Narrator: Then Jesus said,

Jesus: Little children, I am with you only a little longer. So, I give you a new commandment, that you love one another. Just as I have loved you, you also should love one another. By this everyone will know that you are my disciples, if you have love for one another.

Silence for Meditation

Sermon (may be based on any of the following)

- How can we show our love for each other, so that the world will know we are followers of Jesus?

- How does this congregation show its love for those in the church family?
- How do we show our love for those in our neighborhood?
- How do we show our love for the world we live in?
- Who is the Source of our love?
- Do we know that we are loved enough so that we might share?
- Where are we being called to demonstrate the love of Christ?

Prayers for the World, That It and We May Know God's Love

Hymn: "What wondrous love is this" U. S. folk hymn

No Benediction—Depart in Silence

3. COMMUNION AND ANOINTING, BASED ON MARK 14:3-9 AND 1 CORINTHIANS 11:23-26

Call to Worship (based on Mark 14:8b-9)

During Holy Week, a woman came
and anointed Jesus' head.
**Jesus said, "She has anointed my body
in preparation for burial.**
"Wherever the good news is proclaimed
in the whole world, what she has done will be told
in remembrance of her."
**Today we remember and learn
from this unnamed woman,
who returned the love of Jesus with her gift.**

Hymn: "What wondrous love is this" U. S. folk hymn

Scripture Reading: Mark 14:3-9
(See also Scripture Presentation on page 18)

Response to Scripture: Psalm 116:12-14

What shall I return to the Lord for all this bounty to me?
I will lift up the cup of salvation
  and call on the name of the Lord,
I will pay my vows to the Lord
  in the presence of all God's people.

Prayer (based on Mark 14:3-9 and John 13:3-17, 33-35)

We give thanks, loving God, for this woman
  who loved Jesus so much that she gave a costly gift
    of anointing and of herself.
She reminds us of the great love your son Jesus
  has for us,
love that he demonstrated on this night by washing
  the disciples' feet, like a servant,
  and then by giving his life for the whole world.
Help us to follow the commandment
  Jesus gave his followers,
to love one another as he loved us,
  that the world might know that we are Christians
  by our love. Amen.

Hymn: "We are one in the Spirit" by Peter Scholtes

Sermon or Meditation (Optional Hymn for Meditation: "Healing river of the Spirit" by Ruth Duck)

Invitation to the Communion Table: 1 Corinthians 11:23-26

For I received from the Lord what I also handed on to you, that the Lord Jesus took a loaf of bread, and when he had given thanks, he broke it and said, "This is my body that is broken for you. Do this in remembrance of me." In the same way Jesus took the cup after supper, saying, "This cup is the new covenant in my blood. Do this, as often as you drink it, in remembrance of me." For as often as you eat this bread and drink the cup, you proclaim the Lord's death and resurrection until he comes again.

Prayer

We give you thanks, Creator of the universe,
that you loved us enough to come in human flesh
   and live among us.
Thank you for the lives you touched and healed
   throughout the ages,
for the teachings you gave to your followers.
Come to us now, in this meal of remembrance
   and of hope,
that we might learn from you and be touched by you.
Bless these elements of bread and drink
that they may carry your love into us
   and into the whole world.
Bless this oil that it may mark us
   as your own baptized children
and strengthen us to do your will,
   following the example of Christ.
We ask these things in the power of the Holy Spirit.
   Amen.

Persons may come forward to receive anointing (by the sign of the cross on forehead or back of the hand, with olive or other oil) and Communion.

Response: "Canticle of Love" The United Methodist Hymnal #646 or "Ubi caritas" from Taizé

Blessing

Go in peace to serve God and your neighbor
in all that you do.
May the blessing of God all-loving,
Jesus Christ who gave his all for us,
and the power of the Holy Spirit go with you
from this time forward. Amen.

4. LUKE 22 AND COMMUNION

Call to Worship: Psalm 116:12, 14-19

What shall I return to the Lord for all this bounty to me?
I will pay my vows to the Lord
in the presence of all God's people,
in the courts of the house of the Lord,
in your midst, O Jerusalem.
Praise the Lord!

Hymn Suggestions

- "Christ, let us come with you" by Shirley Erena Murray
- "Crown as your king the king who came crownless" by Thomas H. Troeger
- "Live in charity/Ubi caritas" from Taizé

Scripture Reading: Luke 22:14, 24-46

Option: Use drama from Luke 22:14, 21-27 and related children's sermon (See Palm/Passion Sunday, pages 27–28)

Confession and Pardon

Servant Jesus,
you taught us by your example how to love
and serve others.

Forgive our grasping at authority and free us
   that we may be content
   in serving you and loving your children.
In the name of the One who sent you, the Source of love.
   Amen.

By the life and death of Jesus we are forgiven.
Thanks be to God.

Invitation to Communion

Jesus ate with his disciples even knowing one would betray, another deny, and many desert him. This meal is open to all of us, as healing for our souls.

Hymn Suggestions

- "Draw us in the Spirit's tether" by Percy Dearmer
- "Eternal Christ, you rule" by Dan Damon
- "Servants of the Savior" by Sylvia G. Dunstan

Words of Institution: Luke 22:15-20

Prayer of Thanksgiving

Giving God, as you came in flesh to live among us
   and show us how to live:
**We remember you in this meal as our
Maker, Teacher, Healer, Feeder,
Redeemer and Sustainer.**
(*Option: Leave time here for persons to share testimonies about the presence of God in their lives or what Communion means to them.*)
   Thank you for giving yourself to us
   so fully in love for us.
**Help us to understand your great love for us,
that we may have full assurance
of your pardon and grace.**

Thank you for pouring out your new covenant
   through your blood.
Help us to live into the promises of that covenant,
   as free and joyful persons,
   sharing your love in the world.
Bless these elements of bread and cup,
   that they may bring us into your presence.
Bless us, so that we may live in the world
   as your children, forgiven and freed.
All: In the name of the Holy Trinity, we pray. Amen.

Prayer after Receiving (based on Psalm 116:12, 14)

What shall we return to the Lord
   for all this bounty to us?
   We will pay our vows to the Lord
   in the presence of all God's people,
   in the courts of the house of the Lord,
   in your midst, O Jerusalem.
Praise the Lord!

Hymn: Stanzas 4–5 of "I come with joy" by Brian Wren

5. HOLY THURSDAY
IN THE STYLE OF TAIZÉ

Songs from the Taizé Community and hymn options are given below, to make these services as flexible as possible. The Taizé Community in France is known for its rhythm of worship, work, and Bible study, with morning, midday, and evening prayer each day. The repetition of simple choruses lays the groundwork for communal prayer, both through singing and as persons drop in and out of the singing for individual prayer time. The options for Taizé songs in this service come from *Songs and Prayers from Taizé* (Chicago: GIA, G-3719-P,

1991) and are also found in many recent hymnals and hymn supplements.

Scripture Reading: John 13:1

- Taizé: "Christ Jesus, Lord and Savior/O Christe Domine" *or* "We adore you, Jesus Christ"
- Hymn: "Blessed be the name," USA camp meeting chorus, arr. Ralph E. Hudson

Scripture Reading: John 13:3-10a

- Taizé: "Give to us your peace/Dona nobis pacem, Domine" *or* "My soul is at rest"
- Hymn: "Dona nobis pacem," traditional Latin round

Scripture Reading: John 13:12-17

- Taizé: "Live in charity/Ubi caritas"
- Hymn: "Jesu, Jesu, fill us with your love" by Tom Colvin

Scripture Reading: John 13:31-35

Silent Reflection on Scripture (1–5 minutes)

Invitation to Communion
(Use words from your worship tradition)

Prayer of Confession and Pardon

In light of your commandment to love one another
  as you have loved us,
    we see our failures to love, Holy Jesus:
We have not remembered or even grasped
  how much you love us.
We have not given that love away,

that you might fill us anew.
We have neglected each other and argued so much
    that the world does not see
        that we are your disciples.
(*Silence for reflection*)
Holy God, forgive us, we pray.
Free us to know that we are loved,
    and to love one another.
Grant us your Spirit of forgiveness.

By the power and work of the Holy Trinity,
    we are loved and forgiven.
Thanks be to God!
As forgiven and beloved children of God,
    let us greet one another with signs of God's peace.

Optional Hymn

Following the Passing of the Peace, a song may be sung while the Communion Table is prepared.
    • Taizé: "Live in charity/Ubi caritas" *or* "Eat this bread"

Great Thanksgiving

Includes sung congregational reponses from "Let us break bread together" African American spiritual
    On this night, we gather
        as the Hebrew people gathered in exile
    to share the Lamb and celebrate
        your passing over them in mercy.
    On this night, we pass on to children and strangers
        what we have received from you, Lord Jesus:
    Who on the night you left us took bread,
        blessed it, broke it
        and gave it to the disciples, saying,
        "Do this in remembrance of me,"
    (*Sing stanza 1: "Let us break bread together"*)

Then at the table with the disciples
   Jesus took the cup and said,
      "This is my life for you,
      share in its newness and remember me."
And so we remember:
   how you came to us, clothed in human flesh,
   how you taught us by living and dying,
   how you fed us in happy times
      and when facing grief.
(Sing stanza 2: "Let us drink wine together")
As we remember you, Lord Jesus Christ
   pour out yourself again for us
      and on these gifts of bread and cup.
By your Holy Spirit make us living remembrances
   of your great love and life.
Fill us with a new understanding of love
   among all your children
   that others may see our witness
      and draw close to you.
We praise your name, Holy God,
   the One who made us, the One who faced death for us, and
      the One who sustains our lives.
(Sing stanza 3: "Let us praise God together on our knees")

Distribution of Communion

Any of the songs sung during the service may be repeated during the distribution of Communion or sing "In the singing" by Shirley Erena Murray.

Prayer of Thanksgiving for Receiving:

Holy Trinity, you have given yourself to us
   through the life and death of Jesus Christ.
With thanksgiving, we go now
   to give ourselves for others.

6. TENEBRAE SERVICE

Tenebrae or "Service of Darkness" or "Service of Shadows" is the name given to a medieval tradition of reading Scripture and extinguishing candles, either at the end of a Holy Thursday service or on Good Friday. This service may stand alone on Good Friday or may be combined with one of the previous Holy Thursday services. Congregational involvement during the readings may be limited to hymns or songs known by heart (for example, the first stanza of "When I survey the wondrous cross") or one of the Taizé pieces used throughout the entire service; there are also suggestions of variations on "Were you there" for singing before the readings. This service calls for ten candles and a Christ candle (also used at Christmas time). Two or more readers should be involved, highlighting the drama inherent in these readings.

Hymn Suggestions

- "Eternal Christ, you rule" by Dan Damon
- "I will take some time to pray" by John Thornburg
- "In the cross of Christ I glory" by John Bowring
- "O Love divine, what hast thou done!" by Charles Wesley
- "O sacred Head, now wounded" anonymous, translated by Paul Gerhardt
- "O the Lamb" nineteenth-century camp meeting song, adapted by Ellen Jane Lorenz
- "O wheat whose crushing was for bread" by Delores Dufner
- "Underneath the present suffering" by Dan Damon
- "We stand amazed before your love" by Sylvia G. Dunstan
- "What wondrous love is this" U. S. folk hymn
- "When I survey the wondrous cross" by Isaac Watts

Taizé Suggestions

- "By night/De noche iremos"
- "Our darkness/La ténèbre"

- "Stay with us/Bleib mit deiner Gnade"
- "When the night becomes dark"
- "Within our darkest night/Dans nos obscurités"

Call to Worship

God is light. In God there is no darkness at all.
Jesus Christ is the light of the world.
On this night, centuries ago, the world attempted
    to put out the light of Jesus' earthly life.
Yet our darkness is never darkness in God's sight.

Hymn (from lists above)

Prayer

God who came in flesh in Jesus Christ,
    you know the shadows of sin and evil.
Strengthen us to follow your light, Lord Christ,
    that it may shine in us as a beacon to your truth.
Through the power of your Holy Spirit we pray,
One God, now and forever. Amen.

"Were You There" (optional stanza variations to sing before each reading)

If used, extinguish candles in silence.
Were you there when . . .
    . . . he knelt alone in prayer?
    . . . they came to take my Lord?
    . . . they stood my Lord on trial?
    . . . my Lord was beat upon?
    . . . denial came from Peter?
    . . . the second trial began?
    . . . the crowd turned their backs?
    . . . the soldiers mocked my Lord?
    . . . they crucified my Lord?

. . . they taunted dying Christ?
. . . my Lord gave up his life?
. . . they laid him in the tomb?

Scripture Reading: Mark 14:32-42

Candle is extinguished (while a hymn/song is sung)

Reading: Mark 14:43-50

Candle is extinguished (while a hymn/song is sung)

Reading: Mark 14:53-62

Candle is extinguished (while a hymn/song is sung)

Reading: Mark 14:63-65

Candle is extinguished (while a hymn/song is sung)

Reading: Mark 14:66-72

Candle is extinguished (while a hymn/song is sung)

Reading: Mark 15:1-5

Candle is extinguished (while a hymn/song is sung)

Reading: Mark 15:6-15

Candle is extinguished (while a hymn/song is sung)

Reading: Mark 15:16-20

Candle is extinguished (while a hymn/song is sung)

Reading: Mark 15:21-24

Candle is extinguished (while a hymn/song is sung)

Reading: Mark 15:25-32

Candle is extinguished (while a hymn/song is sung)

Reading: Mark 15:33-39

Christ candle is extinguished (followed by silence)

Reading: Mark 15:40-41, 45-46

Perhaps read by someone in narthex or off to the side, so that the sanctuary is in darkness

People Depart in Silence and Darkness

CHAPTER THREE

GOOD FRIDAY

INTRODUCTION

This is historically the day when Jesus died on the cross for the intercession of the whole world. It is a day of sorrow for those who follow Jesus, that he should die such a death. It is a day of mourning and meditation, a day of walking with Jesus and then staying by the cross to contemplate and pray. God takes this act of crucifixion and does something absolutely incredible with it, turning it into the day of ultimate forgiveness. Visuals include cross, black or purple cloth, crown of thorns; nothing shiny, other than possibly a cross, should be on the altar. The focus of this day is the cross.

1. SORROW AND PROMISE, BASED ON PSALM 22

Hymn Suggestions

- "A spendthrift lover is the Lord" by Thomas H. Troeger
- "Christ of the sad face" by Shirley Erena Murray

- "Crown as your king the king who came crownless" by Thomas H. Troeger
- "Crucified Savior" by Thomas H. Troeger
- "Eternal Christ, you rule" by Dan Damon
- "Follow the way" by Shirley Erena Murray
- "God weeps" by Shirley Erena Murray
- "Jesus walked this lonesome valley" American folk hymn
- "Kneeling in the garden grass" by Thomas H. Troeger
- "Lord, turn our grieving into grace" by Shirley Erena Murray
- "O sacred Head, now wounded" translated by Paul Gerhardt
- "Shadow and substance" by Dan Damon
- "We look down deep to look out far" by Thomas H. Troeger
- "When I survey the wondrous cross" by Isaac Watts
- "Why has God forsaken me?" by William L. Wallace

Optional Meditations

- "The cross on the hill is the measuring rod" poem by Thomas H. Troeger
- "In the beginning, so the story goes" by Sylvia G. Dunstan

Litany of Trust (based on Psalm 22:3-5)

You, O God, are holy, enthroned on the praises of Israel.
In you our ancestors trusted, and you delivered them.
To you, O God, our ancestors cried, and were saved;
In you they trusted, and were not put to shame.
In time of trial and death, Jesus cried to you;
Like him, we trust you, O God, to save us.

Hymn

- "Jesus walked this lonesome valley" American folk hymn
- "O sacred Head, now wounded" translated by Paul Gerhardt

Invitation to Consider the Cross

For three readers

Reader 1:
> Jesus cried from the cross,
> > using the words of the psalmist:
>
> My God, my God, why have you forsaken me?
> Why are you so far from helping me,
> > from the words of my groaning?
>
> O my God, I cry by day, but you do not answer;
> > and by night, but find no rest. (*Psalm 22:1-2*)

Readers 2 and 3 (responsively):
> This is a time of shadows,
> > when darkness covered the earth.
>
> **This is a time to acknowledge**
> > **the dark night of the soul,**
> > **when even God in Jesus felt separated**
> > **from God's own self.**
>
> This is the time when we walk through
> > the valley of the shadow of death.
>
> **This is the time God wept over the earth.**

Hymn: "Were you there when they crucified my Lord"

Scripture Reading: Psalm 22

Prayer of Lament

Responsive Prayer (based on Psalm 22)
> On this day of sadness,
> > as we focus on your death on a cross:
>
> **Come near to us, O God.**
>
> Make us steadfast as we think
> > about Jesus' life and death.
>
> **Open our hearts to learn of him and thus of you,**
> > **great God.**

Jesus went through trial, rejection, degradation,
   physical pain, and the flight of his friends.
Jesus understands our pain and sorrows.
Truly, he knows, and so you know, great God,
   what it is like for us.
   You walk with us in trials, loss, and grief.
We know sorrow:
(*All or Multiple Voices*)
We know the feeling of being forsaken.
There are tears that will not stop.
Scorn and hatred abound.
Death and destruction surround us.
Evildoers are all around us.
The world is a frightening place.
Floods and earthquakes strike.
People fall sick and die.
Others lose their jobs and homes
Loved ones walk away and don't come back.
Hunger and cruelty exist unnecessarily.

All: **We turn away from you, O God,**
   and the pain is unbearable.
(*Silence*)
You came in flesh, in Jesus Christ,
   to make a bridge for us to you.
   Jesus showed us your love, your mercy,
   and your glory.
In his death, we saw your forgiveness.
   In his resurrection, we learn that you
   will never leave us.
In life, in death, in resurrection,
   Jesus opened the way for all people
   Today we lift the world in our prayers to you.
(*Silence*)
O Lord, do not be far away.
   O my Help, come quickly to the aid of the world.
We will tell your name to our brothers and sisters.

In the midst of the congregation
  we will praise you.
We bring you, great God,
  The people of . . .
  Those ill or in hospice . . .
  Those in hunger and want . . .
  Those caught in the midst of war . . .
  Children whose innocence has been stolen . . .
  Elderly whose hope is gone . . .
  Youth with no place to turn . . .
  Those who feel unloved, unwanted . . .
  Those in power, who make decisions . . .
  Those with money and medicine to help . . .
  Those with gifts to share . . .
  Those who need to know your mercy . . .
O Lord, do not be far away.
  O my Help, come quickly to the aid of the world.
We will tell your name to our brothers and sisters.
  In the midst of the congregation
    we will praise you.
Let your justice triumph.
  Let your mercy be known.
Let your forgiveness heal.
  Let your love be shown.
We know that on this day, when it looks like you are defeated
    in Jesus,
  You are working hard
    for the salvation of the world;
You are pouring out grace in the midst of sin and evil;
  You are choosing us in spite of ourselves.
Help us to move toward you,
  To open our minds and hearts to your will.
O Lord, do not be far away.
  O my Help, come quickly to the aid of the world.
We will tell your name to our brothers and sisters.
  In the midst of the congregation
    we will praise you.

Hymn: "When I survey the wondrous cross" by Isaac Watts

Time for Prayer and Meditation

Optional Hymns for Meditation

- "Christ, your love is overwhelming" by Sylvia G. Dunstan
- "Eternal Intercessor, you plead with arms outstretched" by Sylvia G. Dunstan
- "God weeps" by Shirley Erena Murray
- "Jesus' death was not God's need" by Dan Damon
- "The cross on the hill is the measuring rod" by Thomas H. Troeger
- "This is your coronation" by Sylvia G. Dunstan
- "We glory in the cross" by Delores Dufner

2. SERVICE OF INTERCESSION, BASED ON HEBREWS AND INCORPORATING THE STATIONS OF THE CROSS FROM JOHN 18:1–19:42

The tradition of marking Jesus' journey to the cross—following the Last Supper until he was laid in the tomb—began early in the church's life as pilgrims went to the Holy Land to follow Christ's journey on Holy Thursday and Good Friday. The service may take place inside or outside, with hymns and prayers, with visuals and drama. The prayers remind us that this is the day that Jesus interceded for the whole world. Any of the hymns suggested may be used during the Stations; "O the Lamb" and "Follow the way" may be sung between the readings and the prayer. The "Stations" section of the service may also stand alone.

Hymn Suggestions

- "Acclamations for the Passion" by Delores Dufner, using John version (*sung after each section of the reading*)
- "Because you came and sat beside us" by Shirley Erena Murray (*with refrain, "We ask forgiveness"*)
- "Christ of the sad face" by Shirley Erena Murray
- "Crown as your king the king who came crownless" by Thomas H. Troeger
- "Crucified Savior" by Thomas H. Troeger
- "Eternal Christ, you rule" by Dan Damon
- "Eternal Intercessor, you plead with arms outstretched" by Sylvia G. Dunstan
- "How could a God whose name is love" by Ruth C. Duck
- "In all our grief and fear we turn to you" by Sylvia G. Dunstan
- "Jesus saw the path to death" by Dan Damon
- "Jesus walked this lonesome valley" American folk hymn
- "Kneeling in the garden grass" by Thomas H. Troeger
- "Lord, turn our grieving into grace" by Shirley Erena Murray
- "O Love divine, what hast thou done" by Charles Wesley
- "Spirit of Christ, remember me" by Dan Damon
- "Teach us, O loving heart of Christ" by Shirley Erena Murray
- "We look down deep to look out far" by Thomas H. Troeger
- "What wondrous love is this" U. S. folk hymn

Scriptural Invitation: Hebrews 10:23

Let us hold fast to the confession of our hope without wavering, for God who has promised is faithful.

Hymn: "O the Lamb, the loving Lamb," nineteenth-century camp meeting song

Optional endings:
- To intercede for me
- To intercede for us
- To intercede for the world
- To intercede for the church

Optional song:
- "Follow the way" Shirley Erena Murray

Scripture Reading: Hebrews 10:16-25

Prayer Following Scripture

Amazing God, who has provided a way for us
    to come to you with clean hearts
        and baptized bodies:
Thank you for the gift of Jesus Christ,
    who has opened a way for us to you
    by the sacrifice of his life and death.
May we accept this astounding gift
    with humility and a generous spirit,
    finding ways to live lives of love and good deeds,
    as Jesus taught us.
Grant this through the power of your Holy Spirit,
    we pray. Amen.

THE WAY OF THE CROSS / STATIONS OF THE CROSS
FROM JOHN 18:1–19:42

Jesus in the Garden, Betrayal (John 18:1-8)

Intercessions:
    That we might not betray Jesus, but have God's law in our
        hearts and written on our minds
    For those are have been betrayed by their friends

Taken to the House of Annas and Caiaphas (John 18:12-24)

Intercessions:
> For the leaders of the religions of the world—that truth, justice, and mercy may prevail
> For all who stand trial

Simon Peter Denies being a Disciple of Jesus
(John 18:25-27)

Intercessions:
> Our confession for times when we have not followed Jesus or claimed his place in our lives
> That we might be better friends, encouraging each other to love and good deeds

Taken to the Headquarters of Pilate (John 18:33-38)

Intercessions:
> For the governments of the world—that truth, justice, and mercy may prevail
> For leaders in governments, that they might seek truth

Optional song:
> • "Teach us, O loving heart of Christ" by Shirley Erena Murray

The People Choose Barabbas to be Set Free (John 18:39-40)

Intercessions:
> For all under threat of punishment
> That we might provoke one another to love and good deeds, rather than encouraging the worst in each other

Optional song:
> • "This is your coronation" by Sylvia Dunstan

Jesus Is Crucified on Golgotha between Two Others
(John 19:17-22)

Intercession (may be prayed responsively or by a variety of voices):
> For all who will die this day:

For those who die of hunger,
**that we might do more
to share food and resources.**
For those who die of illness,
that we might work for health care for all.
For those who die from the violence of others,
that we might spread love and teach caring.
For those who die in wars,
that we might work for peace and reconciliation.
For those who die at the hand of their government,
**that other ways might be found to teach right living
and rehabilitation.**
For those who die forgotten or homeless,
**that we might open our eyes
and move to their side.**
For those who die by their own hand
because there seems no way to live,
open your arms, O God.
For those who die when there seems to be no reason,
give peace, O God.
For those who grieve,
give comfort, O God.
For those whose illnesses seem to have no end,
give strength and steadfast love, O God.
For those who see no way out,
give hope and courage, O God.
For those who live with war each day,
give courage and humanity, O God.
For children who live in fear or without love,
give strength and your love, O God.
For those whose bodies are treated
with violence or degradation,
give love and comfort, O God.
For the elderly and those living on the edges of society,
give purpose and strength, O God.
For those challenged by body or mind,
give strength and wholeness, O God.

For those we deem as different and less,
open our hearts and minds and hands, O God.
For those who struggle to do your will,
give strength and courage, O God.
Options for singing or readings for meditation:
- "Christ of the sad face" by Shirley Erena Murray
- "God weeps" by Shirley Erena Murray
- "How could a God whose name is love" by Ruth C. Duck
- "What faith can feel we cannot see" by Dan Damon

Jesus Gives His Mother into the Care of His Disciple (John 19:25-27)

Intercessions:
For all who need care, that they may find
loving and safe places of care;
For all places and persons who have the work of caring,
that they may be filled with love, caring,
gentleness, and mercy;
For us, that we might share the resources we have
of time, talents, and riches.

Joseph of Arimathea and Nicodemus Place the Body of Jesus in a Tomb in the Garden (John 19:38-42)

Hymn "What wondrous love is this" U. S. folk hymn

3. GOOD FRIDAY IN THE STYLE OF TAIZÉ

Both songs from the Taizé Community and hymn options are given below, to make this service more flexible. The Taizé Community in France is known for its Friday evening services where people have the opportunity to light candles and pray around a large cross. The cross may be placed in the middle of the chancel or worship space so that many persons may gather around it at one time. If there is already a standing cross in the sanctuary, candle lighting and prayer may happen there. While this happens the rest of the congregation remains seated and sings and prays.

You may use one musical response all the way through the service instead of the noted responses. Some options are: "Christ, Jesus, Lord and Savior/O Christe Domine Jesu"; "O Lord, your cross/Crucem tuam"; "Our eyes are turned/Oculi nostri"; or one of the many Taizé Kyries.

If you have a choir to assist in this service, try using the Taizé piece, "By your cross/Per crucem," found *in Songs and Prayers from Taizé*. Teach the congregation the first and fourth phrases as their response to each reading. After the third repetition, instruments and/or the choir may elaborate with the other phrases.

Opening Collect

Life-giving God,
    who in Jesus Christ took on human life and death:
Be with us now
        as we consider what you did
            in coming to us and dying for us,
        that we might be with you in all that we do.
In your precious name we pray. Amen.

Musical Response:
- **Taizé** "Stay with me, abide here with me/Bleibet hier" *or* "Stay with us, O Lord Jesus Christ/Bleib mit deiner Gnade"
- **Hymn** "What wondrous love is this" (*stanza with* "*to lay aside his crown*")

Reading: (based on selected verses from John 18:1-5)

Jesus went out with his disciples across the Kidron Valley to a place where there was a garden, which he and his disciples entered. Judas brought a detachment of soldiers together with police from the chief priests and the Pharisees, and they came there with lanterns and torches and weapons. Jesus came forward and asked them, "Whom are you looking for?" They answered, "Jesus of Nazareth." Jesus replied, "I am he."

Musical Response:
- **Taizé** "Christ Jesus/O Christe Domine Jesu"
- **Hymn** "Go to dark Gethsemane" by James Montgomery (*stanza 1*)

Reading from John 18:12-13, 19-21a, 24

So the soldiers, their officer, and the Jewish police arrested Jesus and bound him. First they took him to Annas, who was the father-in-law of Caiaphas, the high priest that year. Then Annas questioned Jesus about his disciples and about his teaching. Jesus answered, "I have spoken openly to the world; I have always taught in synagogues and in the temple, where all the Jews come together. I have said nothing in secret. Why do you ask me?" Then Annas sent him bound to Caiaphas the high priest.

Musical Response:
- **Taizé** "Within our darkest night/Dans, nos obscurités"
- **Hymn** "Jesus walked this lonesome valley/Jesus went and stood his trial"

Adaptation of John 18:15-18, 25-27

Meanwhile Simon Peter was asked once in the courtyard of Annas's house and twice around a fire, outside the place of Caiaphas, if he was a disciple of Jesus. Three times, Simon Peter denied that he was a follower of Jesus, and as he said the words that third time, the rooster crowed.

Musical Response:
- **Taizé** "Kyrie Eleison/Lord, have mercy"
- **Hymn** "Ah, holy Jesus" by Johann Heermann, trans. Robert Bridges (*stanza which begins "Who was the guilty?"*)

Reading from John 18:28, 33-37a; 14:6

For four readers (Narrator, Pilate, Jesus, Voice)

Narrator: Early in the morning, they took Jesus from Caiaphas to Pilate's headquarters. Then Pilate asked Jesus,

Pilate: Are you the King of the Jews?

Jesus: Do you ask this on your own, or did others tell you about me?

Pilate: I am not a Jew, am I? Your own nation and the chief priests have handed you over to me. What have you done?

Jesus: My kingdom is not from this world. If my kingdom were from this world, my followers would be fighting to keep me from being handed over. But as it is, my kingdom is not from here.

Pilate: So you are a king?

Jesus: You say that I am a king. Yet, for this I was born, and for this I came into the world: to testify to the truth. Everyone who belongs to the truth listens to my voice.

Pilate: What is truth? *(Pause)*

Voice: *(off to the side)* I am the Way, the Truth, and the Life.

Musical Response:

- **Taizé** "Christ Jesus/O Christe Domine Jesu"
- **Hymn** "Come, my way, my truth, my life" by George Herbert *(could be solo version by R. Vaughan Williams)*

Reading from John 18:37b-40

After Pilate had said this, he went out to the people again and told them, "I find no case against him. But you have a custom that I release someone for you at the Passover. Do you want me to release for you Jesus, the King of the Jews?" They shouted in reply, "Not this man, but Barabbas!" Barabbas was a bandit.

Musical Response:
- **Taizé** "Lord, have mercy/Kyrie Eleison"
- **Hymn** "What wondrous love is this" *(stanza with "to bear the dreadful curse")*

Reading from John 19:9, 12

Pilate entered his headquarters again and asked Jesus, "Where are you from?" But Jesus gave him no answer. Pilate tried to release Jesus, but the people cried out, "If you release this man, you are no friend of the emperor because anyone who claims to be a king sets himself against the emperor."

Musical Response:
- **Taizé** "Lord, have mercy/Kyrie Eleison"
- **Hymn** "Go to dark Gethsemane" *(stanza 2, "See him at the judgment hall")* *or* "He never said a mumbalin' word"

Reading from John 19:14-15a, 16

Now it was the day of Preparation for the Passover, about noon. Pilate said to the people, "Here is your King!" They cried out, "Away with him! Crucify him!" Then Pilate handed Jesus over to them to be crucified.

Musical Response:
- **Taizé** "Lord, have mercy/Kyrie Eleison"
- **Hymn** "Were you there when they crucified my Lord?"

Reading from John 19:17-20

So they took Jesus; and carrying the cross by himself, he went out to what is called The Place of the Skull, which in Hebrew is called Golgotha. There they crucified Jesus, between two others, one on either side. Pilate had an inscription written and put on the cross. It read, "Jesus of Nazareth, the King of the Jews." Many people read this inscription, because the place where Jesus was crucified was near the city; and it was written in Hebrew, in Latin, and in Greek.

Musical Response:
- **Taizé** "Lord, have mercy/Kyrie Eleison"
- **Hymn** "Were you there when they nailed him to the tree?"

Reading from John 19:25b-27

Meanwhile, standing near the cross of Jesus were his mother, his mother's sister, Mary the wife of Clopas, and Mary Magdalene. When Jesus saw his mother and the disciple whom he loved standing beside her, he said to his mother, "Woman, here is your son." Then he said to the disciple, "Here is your mother." And from that moment the disciple took her into his own home.

Musical Response:
- **Taizé** "Bless the Lord, my soul"
- **Hymn** "When I survey the wondrous cross" *(first 2 stanzas)*

Reading from John 19:28-30

After this, when Jesus knew that all was now finished, he said, "I am thirsty." A jar full of sour wine was standing there. So they put a sponge full of the wine on a branch and held it to his mouth. When Jesus had received the wine, he said, "It is finished." Then he bowed his head and gave up his spirit.

Musical Response:
- **Taizé** "Our darkness is never darkness/La ténèbre"
- **Hymn** "When I survey the wondrous cross" *(last 2–3 stanzas)*

Reading from John 19:31, 33-34

Since it was the day of Preparation for Passover, they did not want the bodies left on the cross during the Sabbath. When they came to Jesus and saw that he was already dead, one of the soldiers pierced his side with a spear, and at once blood and water came out.

Musical Response:
- **Taizé** "Lord, have mercy/Kyrie Eleison"
- **Hymn** "Were you there when they pierced him in the side?"

Reading from John 19:38-42

After this, Joseph of Arimathea, who was secretly a disciple of Jesus, asked Pilate to let him take away the body of Jesus. Pilate gave him permission; so Joseph came and removed the body of Jesus. Nicodemus also came, bringing a mixture of myrrh and aloes, weighing about a hundred pounds. Joseph and Nicodemus took the body of Jesus and wrapped it with the spices in linen cloths, according to the burial customs. There was a garden in the place where Jesus was crucified, and in the garden there was a new tomb in which no one had ever been laid. And so, because it was the day of Preparation for Passover, and the tomb was nearby, Joseph and Nicodemus laid Jesus there.

Musical Response:
- **Taizé** "Wait for the Lord" *or* "Nothing can trouble/Nada te turbe"
- **Hymn** "Were you there when they laid him in the tomb?"

Optional Meditation Suggestions

- "Faithful cross, O tree of beauty" by Delores Dufner
- "Here hangs a man discarded" by Brian Wren
- "In the beginning, so the story goes" by Sylvia G. Dunstan
- "Jesus saw the path to death" by Dan Damon
- "Jesus' death was not God's need" by Dan Damon
- "Kneeling in the garden grass" by Thomas H. Troeger
- "The cross on the hill is the measuring rod" by Thomas H. Troeger
- "Will God be Judge, and will there be a time" by Dan Damon

Prayer around the Cross

Singing continues with any of the songs used in the service. Persons may leave as needed. No benediction in this service as it is part of the three-day (Triduum) event.

A NOTE ON HOLY SATURDAY

Provide one of the prayers from this week or one of the hymn texts to the congregation for their own meditation for this day.

GLOSSARY

Colors, Liturgical. There are traditionally colors designated for the various seasons and holy days of the Christian or liturgical year. The color for Lent is purple, for the royalty of Jesus Christ and for our penitence or repentance of our sins. The color for Good Friday is black.

Good Friday. This is sometimes called God's Friday, because of the important work God did for us through Jesus Christ on the cross. This is the day that Jesus was crucified, interceding for the sins of the world and opening an everlasting way to God for all creation.

Holy Week. The most important week of the Christian year, from Palm/Passion Sunday through Holy Thursday and Good Friday, up through Holy Saturday, but not including resurrection. The events of the life of Jesus Christ in this week are: his triumphal entry into Jerusalem, his final teaching of the disciples, his anointing by a woman, the last meal with his disciples, Jesus washing the feet of the disciples, his betrayal after praying in a garden, trials with religious and political leaders, crucifixion and burial.

Holy Thursday. This day in Holy Week is sometimes called Maundy Thursday, from the new commandment that Jesus gives the disciples to love one another. This day commemorates Jesus' final meal with his disciples, his washing of their feet, and the beginning of his trials by religious and political leaders.

Lectionary. A schedule of Scripture readings for worship, attempting to cover the various books and lessons in the Bible. In the Revised Common Lectionary, readings are scheduled over a three-year cycle, with lessons from the Old Testament, Psalms, Epistles, and Gospels for each Sunday and holy day.

Lent. The season of preparation for Easter and, in the early church, for baptism. It begins with Ash Wednesday and continues through five Sundays in Lent, Palm/Passion Sunday, Holy Thursday, and Good Friday. Its count of forty days, echoing Jesus' forty days of temptation in the wilderness, does not include Sundays.

Liturgy. Originally meant the work of the people, done on behalf of others. This is the work we do in worship each time, gathering as God's people and seeking to become better witnesses of God's love and grace in the world.

Palms. Branches cut down by the followers of Jesus and laid before him as he rode triumphantly into Jerusalem days before his death. This is an exciting time, when Jesus is hailed as the son of King David, coming in the name of God.

Paschal Mystery. The deep mystery of the Christian life, about God's great love for us, shown through the life and ministry, the death and resurrection of Jesus Christ, God Incarnate. We are limited in our understanding of this mystery that contains our passover from sin and death to life and love, but the Holy Spirit helps us to live into it, particularly during Holy Week.

Passion. Though often used to describe only the trials and death of Jesus Christ, the fullest sense of this word is that depth of God's love for us, demonstrated in God's willingness to come in human form and live among us, to teach and heal, to die and rise again, and to grant us the Holy Spirit for guidance and comfort.

Stations of the Cross. A traditional service, originating in the areas around Jerusalem where Jesus was believed to have been taken from the garden, to various places of trial, and then on the way to crucifixion on Golgotha/Calvary. It is generally a service of Scripture readings and prayer or music, focusing on the cross and the work of Jesus in our lives.

Tenebrae. This word literally means "shadows" and it is a service of increasing darkness, most often held on Holy Thursday after Communion or on Good Friday. Candles are extinguished as the story of Jesus is told from the gospels: betrayal, trials, rejection, death, and burial.

Taizé. An ecumenical community, founded in southern France at the end of World War II, which focuses on prayer and reconciliation, particularly ministering to thousands of young people each summer. The contemplative style of daily prayer and singing as prayer developed there has found its way into many congregations in the United States and Canada. The high point of weekly worship at Taizé is the Friday evening service of candlelight focusing on the cross and the work of Christ for us.

Triduum. The time from Holy Thursday evening up until sunset of Easter Day. In the Jewish tradition of counting days, the Last Supper through the Emmaus Road story encompasses the most important times of Jesus' life, death, and resurrection. The first twenty-four hours includes the Last Supper, prayer at Gethsemane, betrayal, trials, denials, and crucifixion. By Friday evening, the start of the second "day," Jesus is laid in the tomb; he is there for "three days"—part of midday Friday, through the Hebrew accounting of Friday evening into Saturday, and into Saturday evening (the third day). On the third day the resurrection happens, as do the visits to the tomb by Mary and the other women, Peter and John, and then the walk to Emmaus and the breaking of bread just as evening falls and the third day ends. The implication for worship is that Thursday evening through Sunday is one long worship service, with the prelude only on Thursday and benediction and postlude only on Sunday. That tradition is not followed in every congregation, but some services in this book are written so as to fit that model.

BIBLIOGRAPHY

Hymnals

Baptist Hymnal, ed. Wesley L. Forbis (Nashville: Genevox, 1991).

Chalice Hymnal, ed. Daniel E. Merrick and David P. Polk (St. Louis: Chalice Press, 1998).

New Century Hymnal, ed. Arthur G. Clyde (Cleveland: Pilgrim Press, 1995).

Presbyterian Hymnal, ed. LindaJo McKim (Louisville: Westminster/John Knox, 1990); also published as *Hymns, Psalms and Spiritual Songs*.

Renew, ed. Jack Schrader, Vicki Tusken, Robert Webber, and John Witvliet (Carol Stream, Ill.: Hope Publishing Company, 1995).

Sing the Faith (Louisville: Geneva Press, 2003).

The Faith We Sing, ed. Hoyt L. Hickman (Nashville: Abingdon, 2000).

The United Methodist Hymnal, ed. Carlton R. Young (Nashville: The United Methodist Publishing House, 1989).

The Worshiping Church, ed. Donald P. Hustad (Carol Stream, Ill.: Hope Publishing Company, 1990).

Worship and Rejoice, (Carol Stream, Ill.: Hope Publishing Company, 2001).

Taizé Resources

Songs and Prayers from Taizé (Chicago: GIA Publications, 1991). Accompaniment and instrumental editions are available from GIA.

Worship Feast: 20 Complete Services in the Spirit of Taizé (Nashville: Abingdon, 2004). While this resource does not include a Holy Week service, it is useful for those wanting to further explore the style of Taizé. CD with split-tracks included.

Single-Author Collections

Damon, Dan. *Faith Will Sing: Twenty-four New Hymns* (Carol Stream, Ill.: Hope Publishing Company, 1993).

————. *The Sound of Welcome: Twenty-five New Hymns* (Carol Stream, Ill.: Hope Publishing Company, 1998).

Duck, Ruth C. *Circles of Care: Hymns and Songs* (Cleveland: The Pilgrim Press, 1998).

————. *Dancing in the Universe* (Chicago: GIA Publications, 1992).

————. *Welcome God's Tomorrow* (Chicago: GIA Publications, 2005).

Dufner, Delores. *Sing a New Church* (Portland, Ore.: Oregon Catholic Press, 1994).

————. *The Glimmer of Glory in Song* (Chicago: GIA Publications, 2003).

Dunstan, Sylvia G. *In Search of Hope and Grace: 40 Hymns and Gospel Songs* (Chicago: GIA Publications, 1991).

————. *Where the Promise Shines: 17 New Hymns* (Chicago: GIA Publications, 1995).

Marshall, Jane. *What Gift Can We Bring?* (Colfax, N.C.: Wayne Leupold Editions, 2003). Includes texts by John Thornburg.

Murray, Shirley Erena. *Every Day in Your Spirit* (Carol Stream, Ill.: Hope Publishing Company, 1996).

————. *In Every Corner Sing* (Carol Stream, Ill.: Hope Publishing Company, 1992).

————. *Sing for Peace: The Hymns of Shirley Erena Murray set to the Tunes of Jane Marshall and Carlton R. Young* (Nashville: Abingdon, 2004).

Thornburg, John, and Jane Marshall. *Can God Be Seen in Other Ways: Hymns and Tunes for Today* (Nashville: Abingdon, 2003).

Troeger, Thomas H. *Above the Moon Earth Rises: Hymn Texts, Anthems, and Poems for a New Creation.* (New York: Oxford University Press, 2002).

———. *Borrowed Light: Hymn texts, prayers, and poems* (New York: Oxford University Press, 1994).

Wren, Brian. *Piece Together Praise: A Theological Journey. Poems and Collected Hymns Thematically Arranged* (Carol Stream, Ill.: Hope Publishing Company, 1996).

SCRIPTURE INDEX